CROSS OVER INTO GAELIC WITH MAGGIE MIDGE AND THE INDEPENDENCE REFERENDUM
REIFREANN NEO-EISIMEILEACHD

by
Rab McPhee

illustrated by
Elfreda Crehan

Gaelic by Steafan MacRisnidh
Maggie's voice: Mairi Iseabail Weir

published 2012 by Lexus Ltd
60 Brook Street, Glasgow G40 2AB

All rights reserved. No part of this publication may be reproduced or stored in any form without permission from Lexus Ltd, except for the use of short sections in reviews.

British Library Cataloguing in Publication Data.

A catalogue record for this book is available from the British Library.

ISBN: 9781904737254

© Lexus Ltd, 2012

www.lexusforlanguages.co.uk

Printed and bound in Latvia by Inprint

In this little book Maggie tells the story of what happened when the Scottish midges were asked to take part in an Independence Referendum. What a time that was!

The text is full of *bridges*. If you want, you can cross over a bridge as you go along and pick up a few words of Gaelic.

And if you want to hear what the Gaelic really sounds like, you can go to **www.lexusforlanguages.co.uk** and download free recordings of Maggie's own voice.

we will fill the sky

from an old midgic chant

Is mis' a th' ann, Maggie Midge.
It's me, Maggie Midge.

Tha mi a' fuireach ann an Alba.
I live in Scotland.

'S e dùthaich bhrèagha a th' ann.
It's a beautiful country.

There's a lot going on here na làithean sa.
these days.

An cuala tu mu / Did you hear about the independence referendum?

You didn't? **Uill,** / Well, let me tell you.

An toiseach, it was the Nats that called it.
In the beginning,

Though sna làithean ud they were known as the Gnats.
in those days

Le G sàmhach.
With a silent G.

Cha robh an t-ainm seo a' còrdadh riutha.
They didn't like this name.

Tha rudeigin ceàrr air,
There's something wrong with it, they said.

Tha e ro shean-fhasanta.
It's too old-fashioned.

So they discussed this with a lot of PR experts.

Agus chosg iad mòran airgid.
And spent a lot of money.

And finally decided to drop the G.

They said this would give them a ìomhaigh nas fheàrr. better image.

Make them nas nua-aimsireile. more modern.

Agus snasail san fharsaingeachd. And generally cool.

Co-dhiù. Anyhow.

The Nats wanted a

reifreann air neo-eisimeileachd. referendum on independence.

Carson? Why?

Deagh cheist. Good question.

Because the Nats said that *a h-uile duine* / everyone would be better off if they were *neo-eisimeileach.* / independent.

We were *mòr gu leòr* / big enough to be able to stand on our own six feet.

Às aonais nan Sasannach / Without the English or *a' chòrr de* / the rest of the United Midgedom.

Gu pearsanta, / Personally, I'd always thought we midgies were *caran neo-eisimeileach* / pretty independent anyhow.

Now the Nats knew they couldn't win gun chuideachadh / without help from us midges.

A chionn 's / Because there are billions of midges and a-mhàin / only some 2 million Nats.

So dh'aontaich sinne, na meanbh-chuileagan, cuideachadh.
we midgies agreed to help.
Gun dragh.
No problem.

But one other group *nach robh ro chinnteach:* wasn't too sure:

the Clegs.*

Bha iad eadar dà bharail.
They couldn't make their minds up.

* *in case you didn't know, a cleg is a word we Scots midgies use for a horsefly*

But the Nats were *glic.* clever.

They knew that the Clegs *dèidheil air* had a liking for that G that *iad fhèin* they themselves had dropped.

You can have the G if you vote with us, said the Nats.

Làn dìth ur beatha.
It's all yours.

So the Clegs talked to their PR people.

Airson grunn sheachdainean.
For several weeks.

And renamed themselves **New Cleggs**.

Much cooler that way, said the Cleggs: the double G gives a sense of

traidisean agus earbsa.
tradition and dependability.

Gasta.
Excellent.

So. The day of the Independence Referendum was agreed.

Midgesummer day.

Gun teagamh.
Of course.

Polling booths were to be open *o mhoch gu dubh.*
from dawn to dusk.

Mar a tha fhios agad, midges only normally come out tràth sa mhadainn in the early morning and at twilight.

And then only if it's ceòthach no mùgach no gruamach. misty or muggy or overcast.

What the Nats really didn't want was latha snog grianach. a nice sunny day.

A chionn 's gur lugha air meanbh-chuileagan deàrrsadh grèine.
Because midges hate bright sunshine.

The day of the referendum came.

Great excitement.
An dùthaich gu lèir was abuzz.
The whole country

Agus bheil fhios agad dè?
And you know what?

Seadh, tha sin ceart.
Yes, that's right.

You've guessed it.

A' ghrian came bursting up over the horizon.
The sun

Like the big ball of yellow fire that it is.

Gun sgòth anns an adhar.
Not a cloud in the sky.

And dh'fhan na meanbh-chuileagan uile aig an taigh
all the midgies stayed at home
during the daytime.

Well 99.9% of them.

Tha e cho teth!
It's so hot!

But the vote went ahead.

With tòrr / lots of Nats and Cleggs and others.

Bha e teann.
It was close.

Ach air a' cheann thall
But in the end
and, in spite of the very low
midge turnout, the Nats and
the Cleggs had their midgority.

And so Scotland was about to start out on the road to finding out what Independence means.

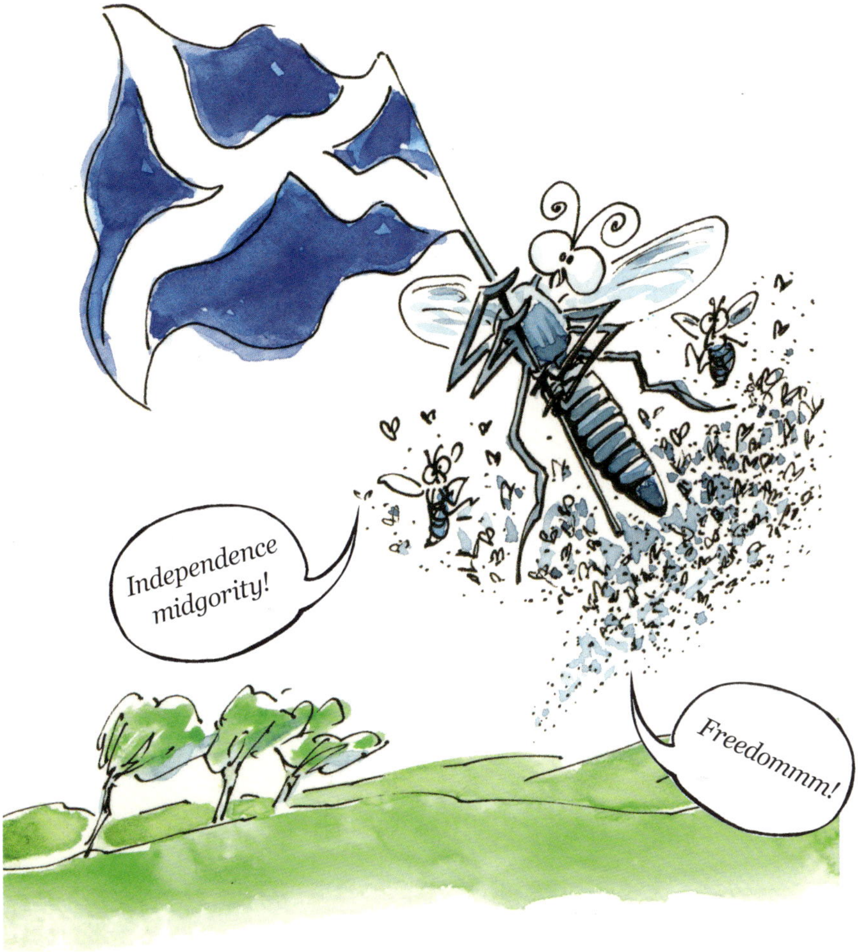

"Independence midgority!"

"Freedommmm!"

Ò thì! Ò thì! Ò thì!
Oh no! Oh no! Oh no!

There was an objection.

Who from? A *Daol-bhreac* ladybird from the ladybird anti-independence *buidheann.* group.

Dè an duilgheadas a bh' ann?
What was the problem?

B' e an duilgheadas a' cheist.
The problem was the question.

The question that had been voted on.

It was this:

Nach eil thu ag iarraidh to be independent from
Do you not want

The United Midgedom?

Well, you might think the question was soilleir gu leòr.
clear enough.

But this ladybird didn't.

No way.

No,

    I do not want

        to be independent from The United Midgedom

is a NO VOTE.

And

Yes,

    I do not want

        to be independent from The United Midgedom

is **BHÒT CHAN EADH** *cuideachd.*
a NO VOTE too.

So, there were in fact no BHÒTAICHEAN SEADH at all!
YES VOTES

Cha robh aon.
Not a single one.

ÙUUUBH!
AAARRRGGGHH!

Abair bùrach!
What a disaster!

The whole affair was discussed

and discussed.

Bha a h-uile duine tro-chèile.
Everyone was confused.

Mu dheireadh, Finally, we had to go to cùirt. court.

And a very senior tarbh-nathrach, dragonfly, the highest judge in all of Scotland, said ...

Dè tha sin a' ciallachadh?
What does that mean?

Tha e a' ciallachadh: thallaibh!
It means: forget it!

Ach tha sinne, na meanbh-chuileagan,
But we midges
caran neo-eisimeileach fhathast.
are still pretty independent.

Mar sin leat an-dràsta!
Bye for now!